INSIDE THE **NFL**

D0930433

Arizona
Cardinals

BY
ZACH WYNER

MEDIA ENHANCED BOOKS
AV²
BY WEIGL™

AV² provides enriched content that supplements and complements this book. Weigl's AV² books strive to create inspired learning and engage young minds in a total learning experience.

Your AV² Media Enhanced books come alive with...

Audio
Listen to sections of the book read aloud.

Video
Watch informative video clips.

Embedded Weblinks
Gain additional information for research.

Try This!
Complete activities and hands-on experiments.

Key Words
Study vocabulary, and complete a matching word activity.

Quizzes
Test your knowledge.

Slide Show
View images and captions, and prepare a presentation.

... and much, much more!

Go to **www.av2books.com**, and enter this book's unique code.

BOOK CODE

E 8 3 1 8 9 8

AV² by Weigl brings you media enhanced books that support active learning.

Published by AV² by Weigl
350 5th Avenue, 59th Floor
New York, NY 10118
Websites: www.av2books.com   www.weigl.com

Library of Congress Control Number: 2014930844

ISBN 978-1-4896-0782-9 (hardcover)
ISBN 978-1-4896-0784-3 (single-user eBook)
ISBN 978-1-4896-0785-0 (multi-user eBook)

Printed in the United States of America in North Mankato, Minnesota
1 2 3 4 5 6 7 8 9 0   18 17 16 15 14

042014
WEP150314

Project Coordinator Aaron Carr
Art Director Terry Paulhus

Photo Credits
Every reasonable effort has been made to trace ownership and to obtain permission to reprint copyright material. The publishers would be pleased to have any errors or omissions brought to their attention so that they may be corrected in subsequent printings.

Weigl acknowledges Getty Images as its primary image supplier for this title.

Arizona Cardinals

CONTENTS

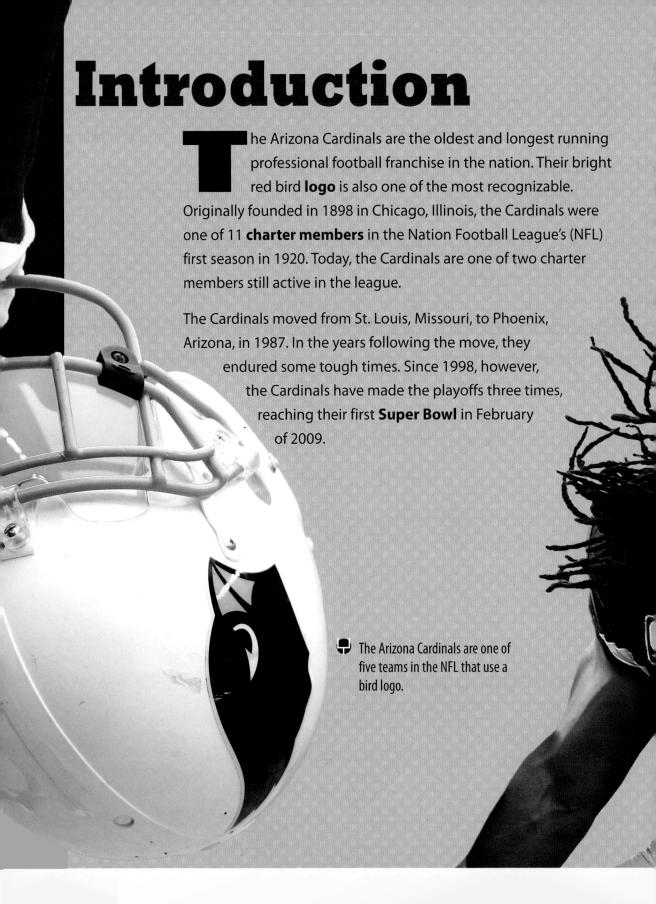

Introduction

The Arizona Cardinals are the oldest and longest running professional football franchise in the nation. Their bright red bird **logo** is also one of the most recognizable. Originally founded in 1898 in Chicago, Illinois, the Cardinals were one of 11 **charter members** in the Nation Football League's (NFL) first season in 1920. Today, the Cardinals are one of two charter members still active in the league.

The Cardinals moved from St. Louis, Missouri, to Phoenix, Arizona, in 1987. In the years following the move, they endured some tough times. Since 1998, however, the Cardinals have made the playoffs three times, reaching their first **Super Bowl** in February of 2009.

The Arizona Cardinals are one of five teams in the NFL that use a bird logo.

Competing for a National Football Conference (NFC) West division title has become a tall order, but with **Pro-Bowlers** Larry Fitzgerald and Darnell Dockett, the Arizona Cardinals can challenge any team. If head coach Bruce Arians can help former Pro-Bowl quarterback Carson Palmer resurrect his career the way Kurt Warner did in the Arizona desert, there's no telling how high this Cardinal team may fly.

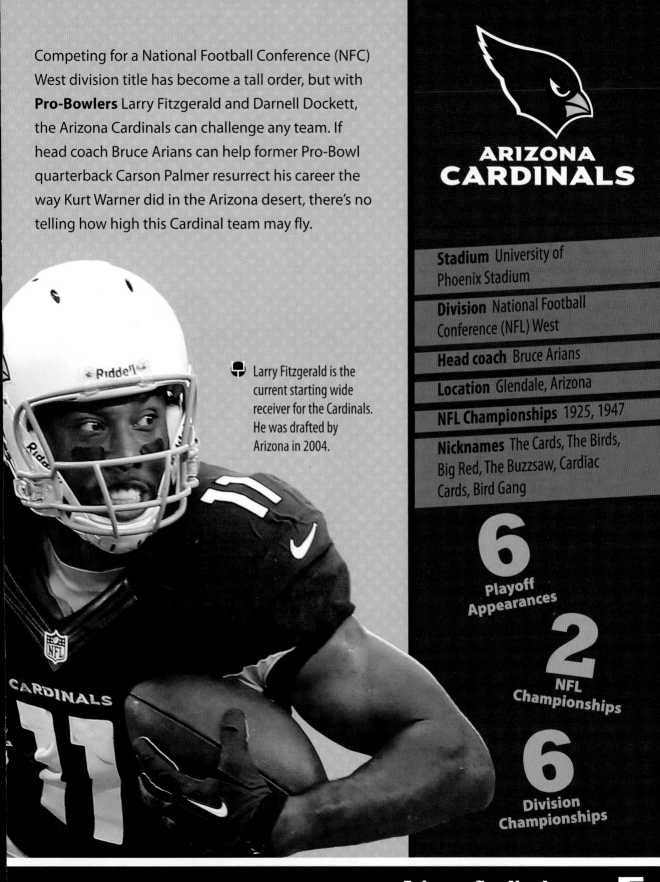

ARIZONA CARDINALS

Stadium University of Phoenix Stadium

Division National Football Conference (NFL) West

Head coach Bruce Arians

Location Glendale, Arizona

NFL Championships 1925, 1947

Nicknames The Cards, The Birds, Big Red, The Buzzsaw, Cardiac Cards, Bird Gang

Larry Fitzgerald is the current starting wide receiver for the Cardinals. He was drafted by Arizona in 2004.

6 Playoff Appearances

2 NFL Championships

6 Division Championships

History

THE TEST OF TIME

The Cardinals are **1**...

...of only two original NFL teams that are still operating today.

When Kurt Warner led the Cardinals to Super Bowl XLIII, it was his third trip to the title game.

From 1920 to 1960, the Cardinals called Chicago home. In 1944, with a World War II depleted roster, they actually combined with the Pittsburgh Steelers to compete as one team. Three years later, the Cardinals, also known as "Big Red," made history. They beat the Philadelphia Eagles in the NFL Championship game and capturing the franchise's second NFL title.

In 1960, the team sought a fresh start in St. Louis, Missouri. However, in the baseball-crazy town, the Cardinals never really caught on. Despite the play of **hall of famers** like Larry Wilson, Jackie Smith, Dan Dierdorf, and Roger Wehrli, they only made the **postseason** three times during their 28-year stay.

In 1988, they relocated to Phoenix, Arizona, yet they remained in the NFC East until 2001. This was a major disadvantage, considering they were forced to endure some of the longest road trips in the league. Their 2002 move to the NFC West made traveling a whole lot easier. Within a few years, Big Red was taking full advantage. In 2008 and 2009, the Kurt Warner- and Ken Whisenhunt-led Cardinals won two division titles and four playoff games. Their surprising 2008 playoff run took them all the way to the franchise's first Super Bowl appearance.

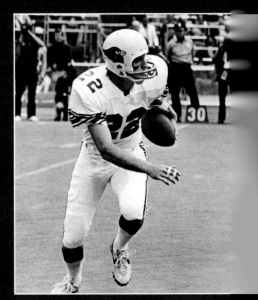

⌐ Roger Wehrli played all 14 years of his NFL career with the Cardinals. In 2007, Wehrli was elected to the Pro Football Hall of Fame.

Arizona Cardinals

The Stadium

University of Phoenix Stadium can seat 63,400 fans.

Located in Glendale, Arizona, University of Phoenix Stadium was named one of the 10 "most impressive" sports facilities in the world by *Bloomberg Businessweek*. It features a **retractable roof** and the world's first fully retractable natural grass playing surface. An opening on one side of the stadium allows the natural-**turf** playing surface to be moved outside the building so it can be exposed to daylight.

⤷ Braving the 125 °Fahrenheit (52 °Celsius) heat, Cardinals fans wear costumes to support their team.

Since opening in 2006, this versatile stadium has hosted more than just Cardinal games. It is the home of the Fiesta Bowl, which is an **annual** college football game that is part of the Bowl Championship Series. It has also hosted WrestleMania, international soccer matches, Rolling Stones concerts, and the Super Bowl. In addition to being fan-friendly, the University of Phoenix Stadium is also eco-friendly. It is a member of the United States Green Building Council and follows strict rules regarding its use of resources. Each year, the stadium generates 120 tons (109 metric tons) of recycled trash. Also, in an effort to save energy, bicycles are used in the facility as an alternate to electric or gas-powered carts.

⤷ While exploring the University of Phoenix Stadium, fans stop at one of its many food carts to sample seasoned almonds and Italian ice.

Where They Play

CANADA

Washington 30

Oregon

Montana

North Dakota

Minnesota 23

Wisconsin

22

Idaho

South Dakota

Wyoming

Iowa

24

Nevada

Utah

14

Nebraska

13

Illinois

29

15

California

Colorado

Kansas

Missouri

31

16

Arizona

New Mexico

Oklahoma

Arkansas

32

17

Texas

Mississippi

Louisiana

12

27

UNITED STATES

Pacific Ocean

Alaska

500 Miles
500 km

Hawai'i

100 Miles
100 km

MEXICO

Gulf of Mexico

AMERICAN FOOTBALL CONFERENCE

EAST	NORTH	SOUTH	WEST
1 Gillette Stadium	5 FirstEnergy Stadium	9 EverBank Field	13 Arrowhead Stadium
2 MetLife Stadium	6 Heinz Field	10 LP Field	14 Sports Authority Field at Mile High
3 Ralph Wilson Stadium	7 M&T Bank Stadium	11 Lucas Oil Stadium	15 O.co Coliseum
4 Sun Life Stadium	8 Paul Brown Stadium	12 NRG Stadium	16 Qualcomm Stadium

University of Phoenix

STADIUM

Location
1 West Cardinals Drive
Glendale, Arizona

Broke ground
April 12, 2003

Completed
August 1, 2006

Surface
natural grass

Features
- LED video displays
- landscaped tailgating area called "the Great Lawn"

LEGEND
- American Football Conference
- National Football Conference
- ⭐ University of Phoenix Stadium

250 Miles
250 Kilometers

NATIONAL FOOTBALL CONFERENCE

EAST	NORTH	SOUTH	WEST
17 AT&T Stadium	21 Ford Field	25 Bank of America Stadium	29 Levi's Stadium
18 FedExField	22 Lambeau Field	26 Georgia Dome	30 CenturyLink Field
19 Lincoln Financial Field	23 Mall of America Field	27 Mercedes-Benz Superdome	31 Edward Jones Dome
20 MetLife Stadium	24 Soldier Field	28 Raymond James Stadium	⭐ 32 University of Phoenix Stadium

The Uniforms

The Cardinals first used a bird in their logo in 1947. It was an image of a cardinal perched on a football.

Many NFL teams use a Ring of Honor to celebrate past greats, often by putting their names on display in the stadium. The Cardinals have recognized 13 legends in their Ring of Honor.

The origin of the Cardinals' name came from the color of their uniforms. The team traces its history way back to 1898, when painter and builder Chris O'Brien bought used maroon uniforms from the University of Chicago for his amateur athletic club team. When presented with the jerseys, O'Brien exclaimed, "That's not maroon, it's cardinal red!" The rest, as they say, is history.

HOME

Since 1960, the Cardinals' uniforms have gone largely unchanged. Their basic uniform design includes white helmets, white pants with red stripes on the sides, and either red or white jerseys. In 2010, the Cardinals debuted an alternate black jersey that was worn with white pants with a black stripe.

AWAY

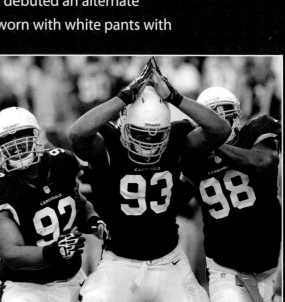

4 Football uniforms have changed over time to become tougher and more elastic. This makes it easier for players to move quickly on the field.

The Helmets

HELMETS OPTIONAL

Though many players used them anyway, helmets were not required by the NFL until 1943.

⌐ NFL helmets are made from tough plastic that can stand up to huge impacts. The first plastic football helmet was designed by a man named John T. Riddell in 1940.

Riddell

The Cardinals debuted their cardinal-head logo when they moved to St. Louis in 1960. Before that, they had opted for a simpler helmet style of either solid red or solid white. Previous to the cardinal head, their logo was a cardinal bird perched on the stitches of a football. However, this logo did not appear anywhere on the uniform.

The face of the cardinal-head logo has changed slightly through the years, but it has never looked friendly. Currently, its head angles down a bit, adding a menacing quality to its eyes. The yellow beak and black feathers around its eyes give this redheaded creature a masked look that makes it look a little scary. The helmet's primary color is white and each player's number appears on the rear of the helmet in black, beside the NFL logo.

In addition to helmets, leg and shoulder pads are required to keep players safe.

The Coaches

5 The number of coaches that have led the Cardinals to the postseason since they joined the NFL in 1920.

These coaches were Jimmy Conzelman, Don Coryell, Jim Hanifan, Vince Tobin, and Ken Whisenhunt.

Before becoming a coach, Bruce Arians was the starting quarterback for the Virginia Tech Hokies in 1974.

Head coach Jimmy Conzelman took the Cardinals from a 0-11 record in 1944 to NFL Champions in 1947. A man of many talents, Conzelman's earlier jobs included major league baseball player, author, and actor. However, his greatest skill proved to be leading men on the **gridiron**. Today, Bruce Arians hopes to oversee a Conzelman-like transformation.

DON CORYELL

Under coach Don Coryell, the St. Louis Cardinals won back-to-back NFC East titles in 1974 and 1975. His offenses were known as "Air Coryell" because of their focus on the **passing game**. In 1975, Coryell's Cardinals were called the "Cardiac Cardinals" because seven of their wins came in the games' final minutes.

KEN WHISENHUNT

In his second year as Cardinals head coach, Ken Whisenhunt decided to start veteran Kurt Warner at the quarterback position. The move paid off. With a receiving core of Larry Fitzgerald and Anquan Boldin, the Cardinals rode the league's third best offense to their first ever Super Bowl.

BRUCE ARIANS

As an **offensive coordinator** with the Pittsburgh Steelers, Arians was on the other side of Arizona's heartbreaking loss in Super Bowl XLIII. In 2012, he took over for leukemia-stricken Chuck Pagano in Indianapolis and was named Associated Press (AP) Coach of the Year. With a champion like Arians at the helm, the Cardinals' hopes are sky high.

The Mascot

At 6 feet, 4 inches (1.9 meters) tall, and with a wingspan of seven feet (2.1 meters), Big Red is easy to spot on the field. Like other NFL mascots, Big Red helps get the crowd pumped before games.

Big Red was hatched in 1998 and immediately took flight at the Cardinal 50-yard line. Shortly after his introduction, he was appearing on the sidelines of every game, tossing T-shirts into the crowd and leading cheers.

Big Red's favorite song is "Bird is the Word" and his favorite book is *Where the Wild Things Are.*

Big Red has benefited greatly from the move to the air-conditioned University of Phoenix Stadium. At Sun Devil Stadium in Tempe, Arizona, he nearly roasted on many occasions, enduring temperatures as high as 125°F (52°C). Big Red is one tough mascot who never backs down from a challenge. Whatever the conditions, he always stays hydrated and cheers with gusto.

During the offseason, Big Red spends countless hours in the gym to stay in shape. He also visits and entertains children in local elementary schools and hospitals.

Big Red's most memorable moments include appearances on MTV, CNN, ESPN, and the Today Show during the mascot convention in New York City in March of 2002.

Legends of the Past

Many great players have suited up in the Cardinals' red and black. A few of them have become icons of the team and the city it represents.

Pat Tillman

A scholar-athlete at Arizona State University, Pat Tillman had his best season as a pro in 2000. He had 155 tackles, nine pass deflections, one interception, and was named an All-Pro by *Sports Illustrated*. Following the attacks of September 11, 2001, Tillman turned down a high-paying contract with the Cardinals to join the Army. Tragically, Tillman died by friendly fire in Afghanistan in 2004. His death was mourned in the United States as the passing of a true American hero.

Position Safety
Seasons 4 (1998–2001)
Born November 6, 1976, in Fremont, California

Position Offensive Tackle
Seasons 13 (1971–1983)
Born June 29, 1949, in Canton, Ohio

Dan Dierdorf

Dan Dierdorf played 13 seasons with the St. Louis Cardinals and was one of the stars on Don Coryell's division-winning squads in the mid-1970s. A big, fast, intelligent, tough, and disciplined player, Dierdorf was a five-time **All-Pro** who excelled as a blocker on both passing and running plays. Under his leadership, the Cardinals' offensive line allowed the fewest quarterback sacks in the NFC for five seasons in a row. The NFL and NFL Players Association selected Dierdorf as the best overall blocker from 1976 to 1978, and, in 1996, he was inducted into the NFL Hall of Fame.

Kurt Warner

After going undrafted in 1994, Kurt Warner played three spectacular seasons in the Arena Football League (AFL). In 1998, he was signed by the St. Louis Rams and led them to a Super Bowl title. In 2005, after being released by the Rams and benched by the Giants, he joined the Arizona Cardinals. Warner struggled through two frustrating seasons but began turning things around in 2007. In 2008, he regained his **Most Valuable Player (MVP)** form, throwing for 4,583 yards, 30 touchdowns, and completing 67.1 percent of his passes. Warner made the Pro Bowl and nearly led the upstart Cardinals to a championship.

Position Quarterback
Seasons 14 (1995–2009)
Born June 22, 1971, in Burlington, Iowa

Anquan Boldin

A star quarterback in high school, Anquan Boldin was converted to wide receiver at Florida State University. The move paid off, as he proceeded to catch 21 touchdown passes in just 23 career games. As a rookie with the Cardinals, Boldin set an NFL record with 217 receiving yards in his first game. In 2005, he and Larry Fitzgerald became only the third receiving duo in NFL history to each have more than 100 receptions and 1,400 receiving yards. In seven seasons with the Cardinals, Boldin made three Pro Bowls and became the fastest player ever to 500 receptions.

Position Wide Receiver
Seasons 11 (2003–2013)
Born October 3, 1980, in Pahokee, Florida

Stars of Today

Today's Cardinals team is made up of many young, talented players who have proven that they are among the best players in the league.

Patrick Peterson

Since being drafted with the fifth overall pick in the 2011 NFL Draft, Patrick Peterson has lived up to the hype. Peterson was an **All-American** at Louisiana State University (LSU) and was widely recognized as the best defensive back in college football. In his first two seasons in Arizona, Peterson made back-to-back Pro Bowls, intercepted nine passes, and became the only player in NFL history with four punt returns of at least 80 yards in a single season. Peterson has blazing speed, and at six feet, 220 pounds, he is big enough take on the game's most physical receivers.

Position Cornerback
Seasons 3 (2011–2013)
Born July 11, 1990, in Fort Lauderdale, Florida

Tyrann Mathieu

A teammate of Patrick Peterson at LSU, Tyrann Mathieu was a two-time All-American. As a freshman in 2010, Mathieu starred in the **Cotton Bowl Classic**, recording seven tackles, one tackle for a loss, two forced fumbles, one fumble recovery, one interception, one sack, and one pass breakup. He continued to impress as a sophomore. On December 8, 2011, Mathieu was awarded the Chuck Bednarik Award, given to the year's best defensive player in college football. His 77 tackles, five forced fumbles and two interceptions made him a finalist for the **Heisman Trophy**.

Position Free Safety/Cornerback
Seasons 1 (2013)
Born May 13, 1992, in New Orleans, Louisiana

Darnell Dockett

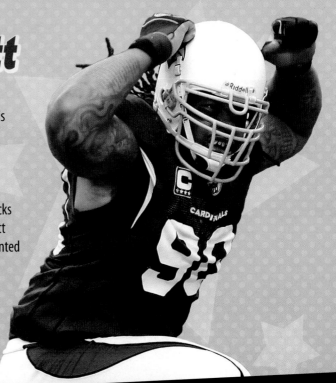

Darnell Docket lost both his parents in a tragic four-month span when he was 13 years old. Raised by his uncle, Dockett earned Maryland Player of the Year as a high school senior. He went on to set the Florida State University record for tackles for a loss with 65. Dockett became the defensive leader of the Cardinals in 2007 when he had 58 tackles, nine sacks, and made his first Pro Bowl. His three sacks in Super Bowl XLIII tied a Super Bowl record. In 2010, Dockett signed a four-year contract extension and stated that he wanted to "retire an Arizona Cardinal."

Position Defensive End
Seasons 10 (2004–2013)
Born May 27, 1981, in Burtonsville, Maryland

Larry Fitzgerald

Larry Fitzgerald is a seven-time Pro-Bowler who will one day be remembered as one of the NFL's all-time greatest receivers. He has led the NFL in touchdown receptions twice and has averaged nearly 14 yards per reception over the course of his stellar career. During the Cardinals' 2008 playoff run, Fitzgerald set NFL postseason receiving records for touchdowns (7), receiving yards (546), and receptions (30). An owner of seven all-time Cardinal receiving records, Fitzgerald has also helped improve the health of current and former professional athletes through his work with the Pro Player Health Alliance.

Position Wide Receiver
Seasons 10 (2004–2013)
Born August 31, 1983, in Minneapolis, Minnesota

All-Time Records

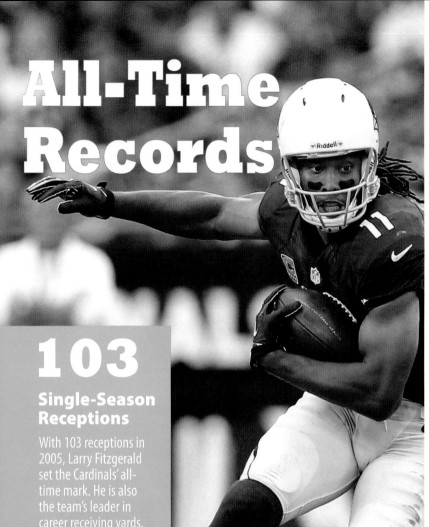

103
Single-Season Receptions

With 103 receptions in 2005, Larry Fitzgerald set the Cardinals' all-time mark. He is also the team's leader in career receiving yards.

1,605
Single-Season Rushing Yards

In 1979, Ottis Anderson set the Cardinals' single-season rushing record with 1,605 yards. That year, Anderson averaged 4.8 yards per carry, caught 41 passes for 308 yards, and was named NFL Rookie of the Year.

45 All-time Coaching Wins

With 45 wins, Ken Whisenhunt is the franchise's all-time leader. His Cardinals made back-to-back playoff appearances in 2008 and 2009.

34,639
All-time Passing Yards

Jim Hart was a four-time Pro Bowler under coach Don Coryell in the mid-1970s. He played 18 of his 19 NFL seasons in St. Louis and threw for a career-best 3,128 yards in 1978.

Single-season Passing Yards 4,614

Neil Lomax captained a high-octane offense in 1984, tossing for a Cardinals' record 4,614 passing yards and 28 touchdowns.

Timeline

Throughout the team's history, the Arizona Cardinals have had many memorable events that have become defining moments for the team and its fans.

1920
The Racine Cardinals become a charter member of the American Professional Football Association for a franchise fee of $100. Two years later, the league changes its name to the NFL, and Racine changes to the Chicago Cardinals.

1932
Charles Bidwell, a vice president of the Chicago Bears, purchases the struggling Cardinals. From 1936 to 1945, the team suffers 10 losing seasons in a row.

In 1960, the Cardinals relocate from Chicago to St. Louis.

| 1900 | 1915 | 1930 | 1945 | 1960 | 1975 |

1898
Painter and builder Chris O'Brien founds an amateur Chicago-based athletic club team called Morgan Athletic Club. Three years later, he buys the used Cardinal-red uniforms from the University of Chicago that serve as the inspiration for the team's name.

1926
With the signing of African American star Duke Slater, the Cardinals become one of the first NFL teams to integrate. Slater is named to six All-Pro teams in his six-year career. He starts in 96 out of a possible 99 Cardinals games.

1982
Behind a high-scoring trio of quarterback Neil Lomax, wide receiver Roy Green, and former Rookie of the Year running back Ottis Anderson, the Cardinals enjoy the first of three-straight winning seasons.

1998
Jake Plummer, the second-year quarterback out of Arizona State, leads the "Cardiac Cards" to their first playoff berth since moving to Arizona. The Cardinals surprise everyone by going into Dallas and beating the Cowboys 20–7, finally notching the franchise's first playoff win. Their magical run comes to an end the next week in Minnesota.

The Future
The Arizona Cardinals date back longer than any other team in the NFL. From Chicago to St. Louis to Tempe to Glendale, Big Red has attracted dedicated fans wherever they have played. Now, with a Super Bowl appearance under their belt, a core of talented young players, and an NFL Coach of the Year at the helm, Cardinals fans can expect consistent wins on the horizon.

In 2009, the Cardinals repeat as NFC West Champions after beating the Green Bay Packers 51-45.

| 1990 | 1995 | 2000 | 2005 | 2010 | 2015 |

Tragedy strikes the Arizona Cardinal family as former All Pro safety Pat Tillman is killed in action in Afghanistan in 2004.

2012
After a disappointing 2012 season, head coach Ken Whisenhunt steps down. During the offseason, the Cardinals hire former Indianapolis Colts coach, and winner of the NFL's 2012 Coach of the Year award, Bruce Arians.

1987
The Bidwell family decides to move the Cardinals away from St. Louis. The team moves into their new home at Sun Devil Stadium in Tempe, Arizona, and changes their name to the Phoenix Cardinals.

Write a Biography

Life Story

A person's life story can be the subject of a book. This kind of book is called a biography. Biographies often describe the lives of people who have achieved great success. These people may be alive today, or they may have lived many years ago. Reading a biography can help you learn more about a great person.

Get the Facts

Use this book, and research in the library and on the Internet, to find out more about your favorite Cardinal. Learn as much about this player as you can. What position does he play? What are his statistics in important categories? Has he set any records? Also, be sure to write down key events in the person's life. What was his childhood like? What has he accomplished off the field? Is there anything else that makes this person special or unusual?

Use the Concept Web

A concept web is a useful research tool. Read the questions in the concept web on the following page. Answer the questions in your notebook. Your answers will help you write a biography.

Concept Web

☐

Adulthood
- Where does this individual currently reside?
- Does he or she have a family?

☐ **Your Opinion**
- What did you learn from the books you read in your research?
- Would you suggest these books to others?
- Was anything missing from these books?

☐ **Childhood**
- Where and when was this person born?
- Describe his or her parents, siblings, and friends.
- Did this person grow up in unusual circumstances?

☐

Accomplishments off the Field
- What is this person's life's work?
- Has he or she received awards or recognition for accomplishments?
- How have this person's accomplishments served others?

Write a Biography

☐

Help and Obstacles
- Did this individual have a positive attitude?
- Did he or she receive help from others?
- Did this person have a mentor?
- Did this person face any hardships?
- If so, how were the hardships overcome?

☐

Accomplishments on the Field
- What records does this person hold?
- What key games and plays have defined his or her career?
- What are his or her stats in categories important to his or her position?

☐ **Work and Preparation**
- What was this person's education?
- What was his or her work experience?
- How does this person work; what is the process he or she uses?

Trivia Time

Take this quiz to test your knowledge of the Arizona Cardinals. The answers are printed upside-down under each question.

1 When did the Cardinals win their first NFL title?

A. 1925

2 Which Cardinal quarterback led them to back-to-back playoff appearances in the 1970s?

A. Jim Hart

3 Who was the first African American player to suit up for the Cardinals?

A. Duke Slater

4 What city did the Cardinals move to in 1960?

A. St. Louis

5 Which Cardinal lineman was selected the NFL's best overall blocker for three straight seasons?

A. Dan Dierdorf

6 Who was the quarterback for the Cardinals' first playoff win?

A. Jake Plummer

7 What year did the Cardinals win their second NFL Championship?

A. 1947

8 Which player is the Cardinals' all-time leader in receiving yards?

A. Larry Fitzgerald

9 Which coach led the Cardinals to their NFL title in 1947?

A. Jimmy Conzelman

10 Which wide receiver for the Cardinals set an NFL record with 217 receiving yards in his first game?

A. Anquan Boldin

Key Words

All-American: a player, usually in high school or college, judged to be the best in each position of a sport

All-Pro: an NFL player judged to be the best in his position for a given season

annual: something that occurs once a year

charter member: an original or founding member of an organization

Cotton Bowl Classic: a college football bowl game featuring a team from the Big 12 playing against a team from the Western Division of the Southeastern Conference

gridiron: a field for football, marked with regularly spaced parallel lines

hall of fame: a group of persons judged to be outstanding, as in a sport or profession

Heisman Trophy: an annual award given to the college football player who best demonstrates excellence and hard work

logo: a symbol that stands for a team or organization

Most Valuable Player (MVP): the player judged to be most valuable to his team's success

offensive coordinator: a coaching staff member of a gridiron football team who is in charge of the offense

passing game: a play in which one player throws the ball to a teammate

postseason: games taking place after the end of the regular season

Pro Bowl: the annual all-star game for NFL players pitting the best players in the National Football Conference against the best players in the American Football Conference

retractable roof: a roof that can move to from an open position into a closed or extended position that completely covers the field of play and spectator areas

scholar-athlete: a student-athlete who excels in academics

Super Bowl: the NFL's annual championship game between the winning team from the NFC and the winning team from the AFC

turf: grass and the surface layer of earth held together by its roots

Index

Log on to www.av2books.com

AV² by Weigl brings you media enhanced books that support active learning. Go to www.av2books.com, and enter the special code found on page 2 of this book. You will gain access to enriched and enhanced content that supplements and complements this book. Content includes video, audio, weblinks, quizzes, a slide show, and activities.

AV² Online Navigation

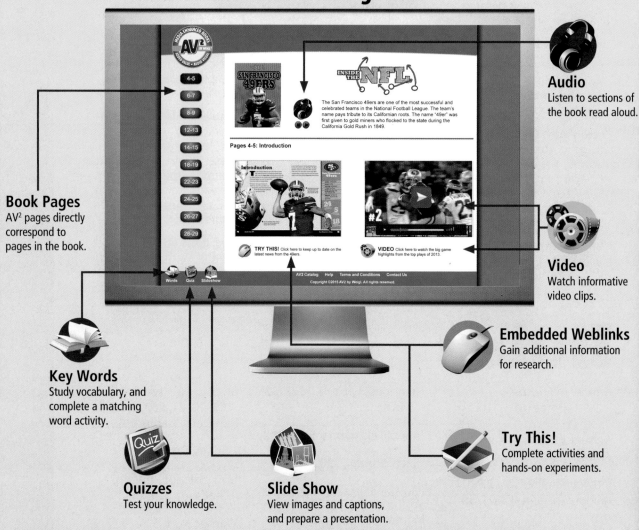

Book Pages
AV² pages directly correspond to pages in the book.

Audio
Listen to sections of the book read aloud.

Video
Watch informative video clips.

Key Words
Study vocabulary, and complete a matching word activity.

Embedded Weblinks
Gain additional information for research.

Quizzes
Test your knowledge.

Slide Show
View images and captions, and prepare a presentation.

Try This!
Complete activities and hands-on experiments.

AV² was built to bridge the gap between print and digital. We encourage you to tell us what you like and what you want to see in the future.

Sign up to be an AV² Ambassador at www.av2books.com/ambassador.